CW00683671

Middl
Rhyming Slang

By James Evans

Illustrated by
Miles Pool &
Des Campbell

Middle Class Rhyming Slang.

First Edition.

ISBN: 9781729379530

Contents

Introduction

Latte sippers. Broadsheet readers. Waitrose shoppers. We all think we know the middle class. We may even consider ourselves part of the much maligned metropolitan elite. But how much do we really know about this mysterious cabal of Downton Abbey devotees? What are they really saying when they witter on about avocados, Grand Designs and prosecco? Last year, in an attempt to get under the well-moisturised skin of this community, I went undercover. I attended more antiques fairs than any person should and drank expensive gins by the gallon. What I found was incredible. A secret language - a middle class rhyming slang. This book offers nothing less than a serious exposé of their vanilla-scented vernacular. It also features cartoons. I hope you find it informative and enlightening.

Ed Miliband - One Night Stand

As in: *"I don't think I'm going to see him again after brunch. But it was a great Ed."*

Origin: This expression appears to have originated from the Greek island of Kos. In 2002 Ed holidayed there with Gary Lineker and Robbie Williams. Gary and Robbie were reluctant to engage in any of the evening antics favoured by their fellow British tourists but Ed showed no such reserve. His conquests numbered in the hundreds, which was no small feat given that the trip was just ten days long. Initially jealous, but then simply bored, Gary and Robbie started referring to his favourite after-dark activity as 'Doing an Ed'. The former Labour leader's name has since become synonymous with this kind of debauchery.

Sourdough Bread - Dead

As in: *"If you've damaged the Aga, you're sourdough."*

Origin: In July 2016 a bakery with a difference opened in Islington. *Nature's Table* promised to be the first 'chemical free' bakery in London. In addition to prohibiting additives and preservatives from its food, it banned soap, washing up liquid and bleach from its kitchen. The food was delicious and the staff were delightful. The only thing that marred the bakery's otherwise stellar reputation were the hundreds of cases of serious food poisoning directly linked to it. When a curmudgeonly health official shut the bakery down, regulars started to refer to its signature bread in grave tones as a mark of respect.

Bonsai Tree - Fee

As in: *"We've been looking for someone to run a wine tasting. What's your bonsai?"*

Origin: Most people swear by their interior designers but none more so than the clients of Jonathan Winterbottom-Smith who is one of the most sought after in the country. He launched his career in 2010 by offering to 'transform any space into one that breathes positivity and affirms your life choices'. Clients were not disappointed. For just £2000 Winterbottom-Smith would turn up, study the room, place a single bonsai tree in the most appropriate place, leave and issue an invoice within 24 hours. The trees not only changed lives but became an an excellent euphemism for discussing that most vulgar of subjects: money.

Falafel Burger - Murder

As in: *"The police have started looking into his death. They think it might have been falafel."*

Origin: It is the dirty secret of middle class vegetarians and vegans across the land. The falafel trade is the most nefarious and bloody in existence. The vegetarian mafia have controlled its production, transportation and distribution since the early 80s, leaving devastation in their wake. Street food vendors and pub chefs that serve the foodstuff live in constant fear - if their suppliers receive a late payment, they may end up with what is known as a 'chickpea face'. If they wish to stop serving falafel, the consequences could be even worse. For this reason, it is not unusual to hear the middle classes associate falafel with one of the most heinous of crimes.

Falafel, She Wrote.

Kevin McCloud - Proud

As in: *"She didn't get into Durham but we're still very Kevin."*

Origin: It's well understood amongst the middle classes that Grand Designs is a near perfect television programme. Viewers are particularly enamoured by the host's ability to sign-off in a compelling way. Kevin McCloud can take any project - no matter how poorly planned or badly executed - look upon it at completion and sum it up in an upbeat, philosophical and even poetic manner. This is a sought after skill amongst middle class professionals who are strictly forbidden from describing their own projects as 'utter shite', regardless of how apposite that phrase may be. When they successfully employ this skill, they are nothing less than Kevin.

National Trust - Lust

As in: *"It was the way she stared at me. I knew straight away it was national."*

Origin: A visit to one of these historic sites can drive a middle class couple wild. Swiping their membership cards together provides the initial rush and this is followed by an erotic journey through the grounds. The ornate furniture in heritage homes seems to act as a powerful aphrodisiac and carefully preened hedges have been known to cause outrageous scenes. The Trust have capitalised on their reputation. In 2010 they entered a official partnership with Durex and asked visitors to 'wrap up' when visiting. A year later they began to hold regular events at their various castle dungeons but this idea was ultimately abandoned when someone got their Hampton Court.

Espresso Machine - Dream

As in: *"I don't think I'm ever going to own a third house. But a man can espresso."*

Origin: Middle class professionals idealise poorly paid and precarious work. Many of them dream of quitting their well-paid jobs to enter the unpredictable world of hospitality. 'One day I'll give all this up to run a lovely little café in Rome' they claim, despite knowing nothing about running a kitchen, providing service nor intending to ever learn Italian. In many homes, small espresso machines sit alongside tabletop pizza ovens to provide a 'Fisher Price' outlet for these ludicrous ambitions. Board any 7am commuter train to London and you'll find yourself surrounded by people desperately holding on to their espressos ...

May all your
espressos
come true ...

Stephen Fry - Try

As in: *"Making your own jam is relaxing and fun. Give it a Stephen!"*

Origin: The middle classes are enamoured by Stephen Fry. This is understandable. But his intellect and soothing presence have caused some to ascribe him superhuman status. The man, they believe, would excel at anything he turned his hand to. Perhaps he would. In any case, when a middle-classer is reluctant to try something, they can be motivated by being encouraged to 'give it a Stephen'. They are briefly imbued with a supreme sense of confidence that propels them forward. The broadcaster himself is above this nonsense and is motivated purely by tea.

Charlie Brooker - Looker

As in: *"I spotted her in Waitrose. She's one hell of a Charlie."*

Origin: Charlie Brooker has gained a reputation as Britain's favourite cynic but in a former life he was anything but. As a model specialising in shoots for health food companies, Charlie was contractually obliged to radiate wholesomeness and positivity. He showed no difficulty doing so, tousling his hair as he smiled at nutrient bars and laughed at salads. His uplifting presence was so well received by the industry that he was featured on the covers of both MyOrganicLife and MyLifeOrganic in the same month - causing him to take a long hard look at what he had become.

He's a

red-hot

Charlie

Granola Bowl - Goal

As in: *"We want everyone who eats asparagus to be using our app. That's our granola."*

Origin: Recent years have been harsh on the Liberal Democrats; in 2010 they jointly ran the country, but in 2018 they are jointly running fruit and veg stall in Hackney Market. As a result, the party has limited resources and in elections, they must prioritise who they canvass. A strategy has been developed; when approaching a door look through the window for potential Lib Dem foodstuffs. These could include hummus, lentils and couscous. At a stump rally in Sheffield, Vince Cable called on party activists to 'go get the granola!'. This has since become their rallying cry.

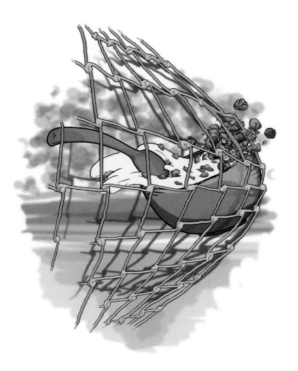

Mary Berry - Sherry

As in: *"I don't really drink. Just a Mary or two in the evenings."*

Origin: In 2012, Henley-based office manager Amanda Stevens decided to hold a monthly 'bake off' to motivate staff. On the first Thursday of every month cakes were served alongside a small amount of fortified wine. After each event it was decided that 'a bit more booze would make the next one even better'. Within a few months, fortified wine was being served alongside a small amount of cake. The bake offs were such a hit they became weekly and then daily occurrences. Today, the staff are some of the most motivated in the UK and the firm has prospered. Although the baking element has been dropped entirely, staff can still be heard asking each other to 'Pass the Mary' every day from 9am.

Another glass of the Mary?

What They're Really Saying ...

Middle Class Translations

Polite Nonsense	Genuine Sentiment
The food is fantastic!	The food is OK.
The food is OK.	The food is dire.
Could you come back in five minutes to take my order?	Could you come back in five minutes to hear this again?
That could work.	That won't work.
Let's put a pin in that.	Never bring it up again.
The job's got a learning curve.	I have no idea what I'm doing.
It was probably my mistake.	It was definitely your mistake.

Polite Nonsense	Genuine Sentiment
We've done quite well out of the housing market.	We are now unimaginably wealthy.
I'm completely broke.	I still have about 10k of savings.
Perhaps my parents could help?	I'll get them to pay for everything.
It was a very mutual break up.	I've basically been dumped.
We don't believe in marriage.	We don't want to get married.
We're a bit on and off.	There's more drama than the RSC.
It's a bit chilly out there today.	I can't stand silence so am saying words.
Don't get me started on xyz.	Let me tell you about xyz.

Ski Break - Fake

As in: *"I'm pretty sure her Jimmy Choos were ski."*

Origin: The middle classes love ski holidays. Once they have checked in, hired equipment and signed liability waivers, they waste no time hitting the bar. They soon befriend other holidaymakers, engaging in deep and meaningful conversations about how cold it is outside and how warm the lodge is. The mountains and lifts are completely surplus to requirements leading some to speculate that they are not actually there, but rather projections designed to make the highly profitable amenities feel that bit more cosy.

Spa Weekend - Lend

As in: *"Money has been so tight this month I might have to cancel Netflix. Could you spa me a fifty?"*

Origin: When middle class professionals get stressed about money, they look for ways to unwind. For many of them, this means heading to the country for a spa weekend. Unfortunately, this is a pricey way to take one's mind off an already financially precarious situation and often involves borrowing money from other anxious middle class professionals. This vicious cycle has turned Britain's once celebrated spa industry into a complex ponzi scheme in which the occupants of one spa are inevitably indebted to those in the next. Its collapse is expected to trigger the next economic crisis.

Stewart Lee - Wee

As in: *"That IPA has gone right through me. Just going for a Stewart!"*

Origin: Few things come close to the relief that one can get from prolonged urination. But for middle class comedy fans, there is someone who can provide this level of satisfaction through well-constructed routines. Stewart Lee mocks his audience with frequent references to their class and social status. Fans are delighted by being identified as middle class and feel gracious in laughing at their own idiosyncrasies. Stewart alleviates anxieties and provides a contentment rarely enjoyed outside of bathrooms. The author of this book can but dream of doing the same.

Get out of my way!

I need a Stewart!

Picnic Rug - Hug

As in: *"I'm really sorry about your Bitcoin. Do you need a picnic?"*

Origin: Middle class people have a difficult relationship with intimacy and many couples are adverse to showing any physical affection towards their significant other in public. A picnic rug, however, provides a sanctuary for those embarrassed by public displays of affection. Shielded by the invisible walls that they believe the rug provides, and encouraged by a sense of luxury that can only be afforded by laying a thin layer of fabric down on wet grass, an otherwise unthinkable embrace is made possible. Unfortunately, some couples find this setup far too comfortable and what follows accounts for 72% of arrests in Surrey's public parks.

Ceramic Mugs - Drugs

As in: *"I've got a killer headache this morning. Must have been the ceramics."*

Origin: Internet shopping allows the middle classes to purchase essentials like organic hummus and Michael McIntyre DVDs at the touch of a button. But for the shopper who has indulged in one too many bellinis it can be a minefield as Julie Smith, organiser of the Cheltenham florists' coffee morning, learned the hard way. In attempting to order six ceramic mugs from John Lewis, Julie instead purchased six grammes of MDMA from a dealer of the same name. The coffee mornings were never the same.

DON'T
DO
CERAMICS

Prosecco Brunch - Punch

As in: *"When he started criticising Game of Thrones I wanted to prosecco him."*

Origin: This unfortunate abbreviation can be traced back to a Carluccio's in Exeter. Two well-to-do couples enjoyed a boozy breakfast together but when the bill came both insisted on paying. An argument ensued and the atmosphere became tense. A waiter suggested simply splitting the bill but by this point the diners were standing and there was far more at stake. Unfortunately, it came to blows. Canvas bags were hurled and floral shirts were badly torn. When the couples were finally restrained it became clear that nobody had been seriously hurt but the breakfast had been ruined. Each couple made a note to remove the other from their Christmas card list.

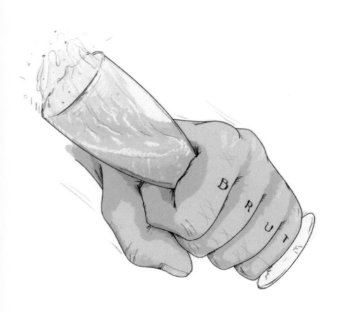

David Mitchell - Ritual

As in: *"I never leave the house without completing my morning David."*

Origin: Flick through TV channels, turn on a radio, or open a newspaper and it won't be long until you encounter David Mitchell. The man is as ubiquitous as he is funny and a hero of the middle classes. But he would achieve far less without his morning routine. A forty-five minute yoga session is followed by a twenty-five minute exfoliation, topped off by either Gregorian chanting or a free-form dance if there has been a full moon. Ritual has become so important to the Peep Show star's wit that he and the term are now inextricably intertwined.

I am not going
on stage
before finishing
my David.

Avocado Toast - Post

As in: *"John Lewis are going to send it in the avocado."*

Origin: In 2012 a young couple in London decided to give up their avocado toast and save for a house. Depriving themselves of this trendy treat alongside nights out, new clothes, cinema tickets and running water allowed them to save for a deposit. After just five years of scrimping, they became proud owners of a studio flat in Zone 12 (also known as Reading). Having successfully swapped fashionable brunches for endless mortgage repayments, they humorously referred to their bills and other letters demanding money as 'avocado toast'. Despite being dead inside, the couple are considered role models and this entry seeks to honour them.

Gin & Tonic - Moronic

As in: *"He's starting his tech company outside of East London. That is so bloody Gin."*

Origin: In 2017, a Bristol bar serving expensive gins offered a free cocktail to all patrons who were willing to Instagram their drink. This was a colossal miscalculation. The bar went bankrupt within three hours and was forced to reopen as a coworking space called 'Doghouse'. (Pets are not allowed on the premises.) The landlord bankrupted his formerly successful business with such wild abandon, he was immediately offered a role in the Brexit negotiations.

Don't be so utterly Gin.

Acknowledgements

Thank you to the wonderful Charis Williams for the support and feedback that got me through writing and producing this book. To Miles Pool for the brilliant cartoons that adorn it. To Des Campbell for the marvellous illustrations on pages 7 & 41. To Jim Jepps for the advice on self-publishing and putting together a half-decent product. To my parents for raising a (potentially Booker prize winning?) writer. To everyone that told me this was a good idea. And thank you, dear reader, for purchasing this book or having a friend/relative that did so. I'm now one sale closer to the deposit on the one-bed London flat of my dreams. Only 500,000,000 more to go!

Printed in Great Britain
by Amazon